CW00417919

KEEP
CALM
FOR
Brides

KEEP CALM FOR BRIDES

This edition copyright © Summersdale Publishers Ltd, 2019

First published in 2012

An Hachette UK Company
www.hachette.co.uk

Summersdale Publishers Ltd
Part of Octopus Publishing Group Limited
Carmelite House
50 Victoria Embankment
LONDON
EC4Y 0DZ

www.summersdale.com

Printed and bound in the Czech Republic

ISBN: 978-1-78685-786-6

Substantial discounts on bulk quantities of Summersdale books are available to corporations, professional associations and other organisations. For details contact general enquiries: telephone: +44 (0) 1243 771107 or email: enquiries@summersdale.com.

KEEP
CALM
FOR
Brides

summersdale

Contents

Marriage

HAPPY MARRIAGES
BEGIN WHEN WE MARRY
THE ONES WE LOVE AND
THEY BLOSSOM WHEN
WE LOVE THE ONES
WE MARRY.

TOM MULLEN

BETWEEN HUSBAND
AND WIFE FRIENDSHIP
SEEMS TO EXIST BY
NATURE, FOR MAN IS
NATURALLY DISPOSED
TO PAIRING.

ARISTOTLE

**MARRIAGES
ARE MADE
IN HEAVEN.**

PROVERB

TO GET FULL
VALUE OF A JOY
YOU MUST HAVE
SOMEBODY TO
DIVIDE IT WITH.

MARK TWAIN

Marriage resembles
a pair of shears, so
joined that they
cannot be separated;
often moving in
opposite directions, yet
always punishing
anyone who comes
between them.

SYDNEY SMITH

ONE SHOULD BELIEVE IN MARRIAGE AS IN THE IMMORTALITY OF THE SOUL.

HONORÉ DE BALZAC

WHAT

COUNTS IN MAKING A HAPPY
MARRIAGE IS NOT SO MUCH
HOW COMPATIBLE YOU ARE,
BUT HOW YOU DEAL WITH
INCOMPATIBILITY.

LEO TOLSTOY

MARRIAGE IS THE PERFECTION OF WHAT LOVE AIMED AT.

RALPH WALDO EMERSON

A GOOD MARRIAGE IS LIKE A CASSEROLE: ONLY THOSE RESPONSIBLE FOR IT REALLY KNOW WHAT GOES IN IT.

ANONYMOUS

I ASKED MY DAD
ONCE, 'HOW DID YOU
AND MUM STAY MARRIED
FOR 33 YEARS?' AND
HE SAID, 'WELL, WE
NEVER WANTED TO GET
DIVORCED AT THE
SAME TIME.'

GWYNETH PALTROW

[MARRIAGE] IS
THE GOLDEN RING IN A
CHAIN WHOSE BEGINNING
IS A GLANCE AND WHOSE
ENDING IS ETERNITY.

KAHLIL GIBRAN

BEING MARRIED IS LIKE HAVING SOMEBODY PERMANENTLY IN YOUR CORNER; IT FEELS LIMITLESS, NOT LIMITED.

GLORIA STEINEM

We don't take ourselves too seriously, and laughter is the best form of unity, I think, in a marriage.

MICHELLE OBAMA

IT IS NOT YOUR LOVE
THAT SUSTAINS THE
MARRIAGE, BUT
FROM NOW ON,
THE MARRIAGE
THAT SUSTAINS
YOUR LOVE.

DIETRICH BONHOEFFER

WHAT

A HAPPY AND HOLY FASHION
IT IS THAT THOSE WHO LOVE
ONE ANOTHER SHOULD REST
ON THE SAME PILLOW.

NATHANIEL HAWTHORNE

MARRIAGE SHOULD BE A DUET — WHEN ONE SINGS, THE OTHER CLAPS.

JOE MURRAY

WHAT GREATER
THING IS THERE
FOR TWO HUMAN
SOULS THAN TO
FEEL THAT THEY
ARE JOINED
FOR LIFE?

GEORGE ELIOT

MARRIAGE IS A
WONDERFUL INVENTION;
BUT, THEN AGAIN, SO IS
A BICYCLE REPAIR KIT.

BILLY CONNOLLY

THE BONDS OF
MATRIMONY ARE
LIKE ANY OTHER
BONDS – THEY
MATURE SLOWLY.

PETER DE VRIES

MARRIAGE IS THE MOTHER OF THE WORLD, AND PRESERVES KINGDOMS, AND FILLS CITIES AND CHURCHES, AND HEAVEN ITSELF.

JEREMY TAYLOR

The sum which two married people owe to one another defies calculation. It is an infinite debt, which can only be discharged through all eternity.

JOHANN WOLFGANG VON GOETHE

A HAPPY
MARRIAGE IS A
NEW BEGINNING
OF LIFE, A NEW
STARTING POINT
FOR HAPPINESS
AND USEFULNESS.

ARTHUR PENRHYN STANLEY

BEING

MARRIED IS LIKE HAVING A
COLOUR TELEVISION SET. YOU
NEVER WANT TO GO BACK TO
BLACK AND WHITE.

DANNY PEROSA

IF I GET MARRIED, I WANT TO BE VERY MARRIED.

AUDREY HEPBURN

CHAINS DO NOT
HOLD A MARRIAGE
TOGETHER. IT IS
THREAD, HUNDREDS
OF TINY THREADS,
WHICH SEW PEOPLE
TOGETHER THROUGH
THE YEARS.

SIMONE SIGNORET

IF EVER TWO WERE
ONE, THEN SURELY WE.

IF EVER MAN WERE
LOVED BY WIFE,
THEN THEE.

ANNE BRADSTREET

A SUCCESSFUL MARRIAGE REQUIRES FALLING IN LOVE MANY TIMES, ALWAYS WITH THE SAME PERSON.

MIGNON McLAUGHLIN

MARRIAGE IS AN INVESTMENT WHICH PAYS DIVIDENDS IF YOU PAY INTEREST.

BOB MONKHOUSE

When a marriage works, nothing on earth can take its place.

HELEN GAHAGAN DOUGLAS

A HAPPY MARRIAGE IS A LONG CONVERSATION THAT ALWAYS SEEMS TOO SHORT.

ANDRÉ MAUROIS

FOR

MARRIAGE TO BE A SUCCESS,
EVERY WOMAN AND EVERY
MAN SHOULD HAVE HER
AND HIS OWN BATHROOM.
THE END.

CATHERINE ZETA-JONES

THE HIGHEST HAPPINESS ON EARTH IS MARRIAGE.

WILLIAM LYON PHELPS

MARRIAGE IS
NOT A NOUN;
IT'S A VERB. IT
ISN'T SOMETHING
YOU GET. IT'S
SOMETHING
YOU DO.

BARBARA DE ANGELIS

HEAVEN WILL BE
NO HEAVEN TO ME
IF I DO NOT MEET
MY WIFE THERE.

ANDREW JACKSON

ONE DOESN'T HAVE
TO GET ANYWHERE
IN A MARRIAGE.
IT'S NOT A PUBLIC
CONVEYANCE.

IRIS MURDOCH

EACH MOMENT OF THE HAPPY LOVER'S HOUR IS WORTH AN AGE OF DULL AND COMMON LIFE.

APHRA BEHN

The secret of a good marriage is forgiving your partner for marrying you in the first place.

SACHA GUITRY

KEEP YOUR EYES WIDE OPEN BEFORE MARRIAGE, AND HALF SHUT AFTERWARDS.

BENJAMIN FRANKLIN

THERE

IS NO MORE LOVELY, FRIENDLY
AND CHARMING RELATIONSHIP,
COMMUNION OR COMPANY
THAN A GOOD MARRIAGE.

MARTIN LUTHER

MARRIAGE IS OUR LAST BEST CHANCE TO GROW UP.

MITCH FINLEY

MARRIAGE IS NOT JUST
SPIRITUAL COMMUNION
AND PASSIONATE
EMBRACES; MARRIAGE
IS ALSO THREE MEALS
A DAY, SHARING THE
WORKLOAD AND
REMEMBERING TO
CARRY OUT THE TRASH.

JOYCE BROTHERS

A GOOD MARRIAGE IS
LIKE A GOOD TRADE:
EACH THINKS HE GOT
THE BETTER DEAL.

IVERN BALL

**IT'S SO GREAT
TO FIND THAT ONE
SPECIAL PERSON YOU
WANT TO ANNOY
FOR THE REST OF
YOUR LIFE.**

RITA RUDNER

THERE IS
NO SUCH COSY
COMBINATION
AS MAN
AND WIFE.

MENANDER

No road is long with good company.

TURKISH PROVERB

LOVE SEEMS THE
SWIFTEST, BUT IT IS
THE SLOWEST OF ALL
GROWTHS. NO MAN OR
WOMAN REALLY KNOWS
WHAT PERFECT LOVE IS
UNTIL THEY HAVE BEEN
MARRIED A QUARTER
OF A CENTURY.

MARK TWAIN

Brides

A MAN'S WIFE HAS MORE POWER OVER HIM THAN THE STATE HAS.

RALPH WALDO EMERSON

IF YOU THINK
WOMEN ARE
THE WEAKER
SEX, TRY PULLING
THE BLANKETS
BACK TO
YOUR SIDE.

ANONYMOUS

I... CHOSE MY WIFE,
AS SHE DID HER
WEDDING GOWN, NOT
FOR A FINE GLOSSY
SURFACE, BUT SUCH
QUALITIES AS WOULD
WEAR WELL.

OLIVER GOLDSMITH

EVERY BRIDE IS
BEAUTIFUL. IT'S LIKE
NEWBORN BABIES
OR PUPPIES. THEY
CAN'T HELP IT.

EMME ROLLINS

THE DEEP, DEEP PEACE OF THE DOUBLE BED AFTER THE HURLY-BURLY OF THE CHAISE LONGUE.

BEATRICE STELLA TANNER CAMPBELL
ON BEING NEWLY MARRIED

It is a truth
universally
acknowledged, that
a single man in
possession of a
good fortune,
must be in
want of a wife.

JANE AUSTEN

THE MOST PRECIOUS POSSESSION THAT EVER COMES TO MAN IN THIS WORLD IS A WOMAN'S HEART.

J. G. HOLLAND

THOSE

WHO BRING SUNSHINE INTO
THE LIVES OF OTHERS CANNOT
KEEP IT FROM THEMSELVES.

J. M. BARRIE

Grooms

THE MAN WHO
SAYS HIS WIFE
CAN'T TAKE A
JOKE FORGETS
THAT SHE
TOOK HIM.

OSCAR WILDE

WHEN YOU MEET
SOMEONE WHO
CAN COOK AND DO
HOUSEWORK – DON'T
HESITATE A MINUTE
– MARRY HIM.

ANONYMOUS

WHEN A WIFE HAS
A GOOD HUSBAND
IT IS EASILY SEEN
IN HER FACE.

JOHANN WOLFGANG
VON GOETHE

MY MOST BRILLIANT
ACHIEVEMENT WAS
MY ABILITY TO BE
ABLE TO PERSUADE
MY WIFE TO
MARRY ME.

WINSTON CHURCHILL

May the gods grant you all things which your heart desires, and may they give you a husband and a home and gracious concord, for there is nothing greater and better than this.

HOMER

A GOOD WIFE ALWAYS FORGIVES HER HUSBAND WHEN SHE'S WRONG.

MILTON BERLE

MEN

ALWAYS WANT TO BE A
WOMAN'S FIRST LOVE. THAT
IS THEIR CLUMSY VANITY. WE
WOMEN HAVE A MORE SUBTLE
INSTINCT ABOUT THINGS.
WHAT WE LIKE IS TO BE A
MAN'S LAST ROMANCE.

OSCAR WILDE

THE CALMEST HUSBANDS MAKE THE STORMIEST WIVES.

ENGLISH PROVERB

BY ALL MEANS
MARRY. IF YOU
GET A GOOD WIFE,
YOU'LL BECOME
HAPPY; IF YOU
GET A BAD ONE,
YOU'LL BECOME
A PHILOSOPHER.

SOCRATES

BUT HE THAT IS
MARRIED CARETH FOR
THE THINGS THAT ARE
OF THE WORLD, HOW HE
MAY PLEASE HIS WIFE.

CORINTHIANS 7:33

NO WOMAN HAS
EVER SHOT HER
HUSBAND WHILE
HE WAS DOING
THE DISHES.

EARL WILSON

DON'T WORRY,
IF YOU KEEP HIM LONG
ENOUGH HE'LL COME
BACK IN STYLE.

DOROTHY PARKER

Have patience with all things, but chiefly have patience with yourself.

ST FRANCIS DE SALES

MY MUM SAID
THE ONLY REASON
MEN ARE ALIVE IS
FOR LAWN CARE
AND VEHICLE
MAINTENANCE.

TIM ALLEN

THERE

IS NOTHING IN THE WORLD
LIKE THE DEVOTION OF A
MARRIED WOMAN. IT IS A
THING NO MARRIED MAN
KNOWS ANYTHING ABOUT.

OSCAR WILDE

Relations

BE KIND TO YOUR
MOTHER-IN-LAW,
BUT PAY FOR HER
BOARD AT SOME
GOOD HOTEL.

JOSH BILLINGS

THE PURSUIT, EVEN
OF THE BEST THINGS,
OUGHT TO BE CALM
AND TRANQUIL.

CICERO

GOD GIVES US
RELATIVES; THANK
GOD WE CAN CHOOSE
OUR FRIENDS.

ADDISON MIZNER

HUMOUR IS
ALWAYS BASED ON
A MODICUM OF TRUTH.
HAVE YOU EVER HEARD
A JOKE ABOUT A
FATHER-IN-LAW?

DICK CLARK

The awe and dread with which the untutored savage contemplates his mother-in-law are amongst the most familiar facts of anthropology.

JAMES GEORGE FRAZER

NEVER RELY ON THE GLORY OF THE MORNING OR THE SMILES OF YOUR MOTHER-IN-LAW.

JAPANESE PROVERB

WHEN

OUR RELATIVES ARE AT HOME,
WE HAVE TO THINK OF ALL
THEIR GOOD POINTS OR IT
WOULD BE IMPOSSIBLE TO
ENDURE THEM.

GEORGE BERNARD SHAW

I DON'T THINK ANYONE HAS A NORMAL FAMILY.

EDWARD FURLONG

JUST GOT BACK FROM A PLEASURE TRIP: I TOOK MY MOTHER-IN-LAW TO THE AIRPORT.

HENNY YOUNGMAN

BEHIND EVERY
SUCCESSFUL MAN
STANDS A SURPRISED
MOTHER-IN-LAW.

HUBERT HUMPHREY

FRIENDS ARE
GOD'S APOLOGY
FOR RELATIONS.

HUGH KINGSMILL

Planning

One has to
resign oneself
to being a
nuisance if one
wants to get
anything done.

FREYA STARK

MIX A LITTLE FOOLISHNESS WITH YOUR SERIOUS PLANS. IT IS LOVELY TO BE SILLY AT THE RIGHT MOMENT.

HORACE

WE
EXPERIENCE MOMENTS
ABSOLUTELY FREE FROM WORRY.
THESE BRIEF RESPITES ARE
CALLED PANIC.

CULLEN HIGHTOWER

THE LESS ONE
HAS TO DO, THE
LESS TIME ONE
FINDS TO DO IT.

ANONYMOUS

The Dress

OVER THE YEARS I'VE
LEARNED THAT WHAT
IS IMPORTANT IN A
DRESS IS THE WOMAN
WHO IS WEARING IT.

YVES SAINT LAURENT

AFTER ALL,
THERE'S SOMETHING
ABOUT A WEDDING
GOWN PRETTIER THAN
IN ANY OTHER GOWN
IN THE WORLD.

DOUGLAS WILLIAM
JERROLD

IT IS DIFFICULT
TO SEE WHY LACE
SHOULD BE SO
EXPENSIVE; IT IS
MOSTLY HOLES.

MARY WILSON LITTLE

A woman's dress should be like a barbed-wire fence: serving its purpose without obstructing the view.

SOPHIA LOREN

A DRESS THAT ZIPS UP THE BACK WILL BRING A HUSBAND AND WIFE TOGETHER.

JAMES H. BOREN

The Wedding

A HAPPY BRIDESMAID MAKES A HAPPY BRIDE.

ALFRED, LORD TENNYSON

BUILDERS, RAISE
THE CEILING HIGH,
RAISE THE DOME
INTO THE SKY, HEAR
THE WEDDING SONG!
FOR THE HAPPY
GROOM IS NEAR,
TALL AS MARS, AND
STATELIER, HEAR THE
WEDDING SONG!

SAPPHO

THIS DONE, HE
TOOK THE BRIDE
ABOUT THE NECK; AND
KISS'D HER LIPS WITH
SUCH A CLAMOROUS
SMACK, THAT, AT THE
PARTING, ALL THE
CHURCH DID ECHO.

WILLIAM SHAKESPEARE

A CLOUDY DAY
IS NO MATCH FOR A
SUNNY DISPOSITION.

WILLIAM ARTHUR WARD

I DREAMED OF A WEDDING
OF ELABORATE ELEGANCE;
A CHURCH FILLED WITH
FLOWERS AND FRIENDS.
I ASKED HIM WHAT KIND OF
WEDDING HE WISHED FOR;
HE SAID ONE THAT WOULD
MAKE ME HIS WIFE.

ANONYMOUS

Hail! happy pair,
whose hearts and hands

United in the
strongest bands

That Heav'n can form,
or love compose,

To sooth the weight
of human woes.

MARIA DE FLEURY

The Reception

A FEAST

IS MADE FOR LAUGHTER,

AND WINE MAKES LIFE MERRY.

ECCLESIASTES 10:19

A GLOOMY
GUEST FITS
NOT A WEDDING
FEAST.

FRIEDRICH SCHILLER

LET US

CELEBRATE

THE OCCASION

WITH WINE

AND SWEET

WORDS.

PLAUTUS

CAKES ARE SPECIAL...
EVERY CELEBRATION
ENDS WITH SOMETHING
SWEET, A CAKE, AND
PEOPLE REMEMBER.
IT'S ALL ABOUT
THE MEMORIES.

BUDDY VALASTRO

IT IS NOT
THE QUANTITY OF
THE MEAT, BUT THE
CHEERFULNESS OF
THE GUESTS, WHICH
MAKES THE FEAST.

EDWARD HYDE

BUGGER THE TABLE PLAN. GIVE ME MY DINNER!

PRINCE PHILIP (AT A DINNER
PARTY AT BROADLANDS)

The human brain starts working the moment you are born and never stops until you stand to speak in public.

GEORGE JESSEL

THE TROUBLE
WITH BEING THE
BEST MAN AT A
WEDDING IS THAT
YOU NEVER GET
TO PROVE IT.

ANONYMOUS

HERE

WE STOP, FOR AN ANGEL
STANDS ON THE THRESHOLD OF
WEDDING NIGHTS, SMILING…
BEFORE THIS SANCTUARY IN
WHICH THE CELEBRATION
OF LOVE IS HELD.

VICTOR HUGO

A WELL-SPENT DAY BRINGS HAPPY SLEEP.

LEONARDO DA VINCI

IF IT WERE
NOT FOR THE
PRESENTS, AN
ELOPEMENT
WOULD BE
PREFERABLE.

GEORGE ADE

THE VERY BEST
IMPROMPTU SPEECHES
ARE THE ONES
WRITTEN WELL
IN ADVANCE.

RUTH GORDON

IN ALL OF THE
WEDDING CAKE, HOPE
IS THE SWEETEST
OF THE PLUMS.

DOUGLAS JERROLD

Love

Love does not consist in consist in gazing at each other but in looking outward together in the same direction.

ANTOINE DE SAINT-EXUPÉRY

LOVE
FLOWERS
BEST IN
OPENNESS
AND FREEDOM.

EDWARD ABBEY

DOUBT

THOU THE STARS ARE FIRE;
DOUBT THAT THE SUN
DOTH MOVE;
DOUBT TRUTH TO BE A LIAR;
BUT NEVER DOUBT I LOVE.

WILLIAM SHAKESPEARE

WHO, BEING LOVED, IS POOR?

OSCAR WILDE

LOVE IS BUT THE
DISCOVERY OF
OURSELVES IN
OTHERS, AND THE
DELIGHT IN THE
RECOGNITION.

ALEXANDER SMITH

LOVE IS EVERYTHING
IT'S CRACKED UP TO BE
– IT REALLY IS WORTH
FIGHTING FOR, BEING
BRAVE FOR, RISKING
EVERYTHING FOR.

ERICA JONG

LOVE CURES
PEOPLE – BOTH THE
ONES WHO GIVE
IT AND THE ONES
WHO RECEIVE IT.

KARL MENNINGER

ONE WORD FREES
US OF ALL THE
WEIGHT AND PAIN
OF LIFE: THAT
WORD IS LOVE.

SOPHOCLES

Affection is responsible for nine-tenths of whatever solid and durable happiness there is in our natural lives.

C. S. LEWIS

FOR, YOU SEE,
EACH DAY I LOVE
YOU MORE,
TODAY MORE
THAN YESTERDAY
AND LESS THAN
TOMORROW.

ROSEMONDE GÉRARD

IF
THOU MUST LOVE ME,
LET IT BE FOR NOUGHT
EXCEPT FOR LOVE'S SAKE ONLY.

ELIZABETH BARRETT BROWNING

LOVE IS A GREAT BEAUTIFIER.

LOUISA MAY ALCOTT

THOSE WHO LOVE
DEEPLY NEVER
GROW OLD; THEY
MAY DIE OF OLD
AGE, BUT THEY
DIE YOUNG.

ARTHUR WING PINERO

WE HAVE THE
GREATEST
PRENUPTIAL
AGREEMENT
IN THE WORLD.
IT'S CALLED LOVE.

GENE PERRET

TRUE LOVE
STORIES NEVER
HAVE ENDINGS.

RICHARD BACH

WHATEVER OUR SOULS ARE MADE OF, HIS AND MINE ARE THE SAME.

EMILY BRONTË

Love makes
your soul
crawl out
from its
hiding place.

ZORA NEALE HURSTON

ARE WE
NOT LIKE
TWO
VOLUMES
OF ONE
BOOK?

MARCELINE DESBORDES-VALMORE

IF

I HAD A SINGLE FLOWER FOR
EVERY TIME I THINK OF YOU,
I COULD WALK FOREVER
IN MY GARDEN.

CLAUDIA ADRIENNE GRANDI

LOVE IS THE
SUBSTANCE OF ALL
LIFE. EVERYTHING
IS CONNECTED IN
LOVE, ABSOLUTELY
EVERYTHING.

JULIA CAMERON

HE FELT NOW
THAT HE WAS NOT
SIMPLY CLOSE TO
HER, BUT THAT HE
DID NOT KNOW
WHERE HE ENDED
AND SHE BEGAN.

LEO TOLSTOY

THE ONLY
GIFT IS A
PORTION
OF THYSELF.

RALPH WALDO EMERSON

LOVE IS
COMPOSED
OF A SINGLE
SOUL INHABITING
TWO BODIES.

ARISTOTLE

MY TRUE
LOVE HATH
MY HEART,
AND I HAVE HIS.

PHILIP SIDNEY

Love is ever the beginning of knowledge, as fire is of light.

THOMAS CARLYLE

LOVE DOESN'T MAKE THE WORLD GO ROUND. LOVE IS WHAT MAKES THE RIDE WORTHWHILE.

FRANKLIN P. JONES

LOVE

DOESN'T JUST SIT THERE,
LIKE A STONE, IT HAS
TO BE MADE, LIKE BREAD;
REMADE ALL THE TIME,
MADE NEW.

URSULA K. LE GUIN

MY BELOVED IS MINE AND I AM HIS.

SONG OF SOLOMON 2:16

WE ARE, EACH
OF US, ANGELS
WITH ONLY ONE
WING, AND WE
CAN ONLY FLY BY
EMBRACING ONE
ANOTHER.

LUCIANO DE CRESCENZO

WHAT A GRAND
THING IT IS TO BE
LOVED! WHAT A
GRANDER THING
STILL TO LOVE!

VICTOR HUGO

Happily Ever After

HAPPINESS IS THE MEANING AND THE PURPOSE OF LIFE, THE WHOLE AIM AND END OF HUMAN EXISTENCE.

ARISTOTLE

I drew my bride, beneath the moon, Across my threshold; happy hour!

COVENTRY PATMORE

LET'S BE A COMFORTABLE COUPLE, AND TAKE CARE OF EACH OTHER!

CHARLES DICKENS

GROW

OLD ALONG WITH ME!
THE BEST IS YET TO BE.

ROBERT BROWNING

IF I KNOW
WHAT LOVE IS,
IT IS BECAUSE
OF YOU.

HERMANN HESSE

OUR WEDDING
WAS MANY
YEARS AGO.
THE CELEBRATION
CONTINUES
TO THIS DAY.

GENE PERRET

If you're interested in finding out more about our books, find us on Facebook at Summersdale Publishers and follow us on Twitter at @Summersdale.

www.summersdale.com

Image credits